Silver *and* *Gold*

Stories of Special Friendships

Compiled by Linda Evans Shepherd and Eva Marie Everson

NAVPRESS

Bringing Truth to Life
P.O. Box 35001, Colorado Springs, Colorado 80935

OUR GUARANTEE TO YOU

We believe so strongly in the message of our books that we are making this quality guarantee to you. If for any reason you are disappointed with the content of this book, return the title page to us with your name and address and we will refund to you the list price of the book. To help us serve you better, please briefly describe why you were disappointed. Mail your refund request to: NavPress, P.O. Box 35002, Colorado Springs, CO 80935.

The Navigators is an international Christian organization. Our mission is to reach, disciple, and equip people to know Christ and to make Him known through successive generations. We envision multitudes of diverse people in the United States and every other nation who have a passionate love for Christ, live a lifestyle of sharing Christ's love, and multiply spiritual laborers among those without Christ.

NavPress is the publishing ministry of The Navigators. NavPress publications help believers learn biblical truth and apply what they learn to their lives and ministries. Our mission is to stimulate spiritual formation among our readers.

Cover design by Jennifer Mahalik
Cover photo by Photodisc
Creative Team: Nanci McAlister, Darla Hightower, Jenny Mahalik, Pat Miller

Some of the anecdotal illustrations in this book are true to life and are included with the permission of the persons involved. All other illustrations are composites of real situations, and any resemblance to people living or dead is coincidental.

Unless otherwise identified, all Scripture quotations in this publication are taken from *The Message: New Testament with Psalms and Proverbs* by Eugene H. Peterson, copyright © 1993, 1994, 1995, used by permission of NavPress Publishing Group. Other versions used include: the HOLY BIBLE: NEW INTERNATIONAL VERSION® (NIV®), Copyright © 1973, 1978, 1984 by International Bible Society, used by permission of Zondervan Publishing House, all rights reserved; *The Holy Bible, New Century Version* copyright © 1987, 1988, 1991 by Word Publishing, Dallas, Texas 75039. Used by permission; the *Amplified New Testament* (AMP), © The Lockman Foundation 1954, 1958; and the *New King James Version* (NKJV), copyright 1979, 1980, 1982, 1990, Thomas Nelson Inc., publishers.

Printed in the United States of America

1 2 3 4 5 6 7 8 9 10 / 07 06 05 04 03

FOR A FREE CATALOG OF
NAVPRESS BOOKS & BIBLE STUDIES,
CALL 1-800-366-7788 (USA)
OR 1-416-499-4615 (CANADA)

This book is fondly dedicated to some very special friends:

Letty — my very first friend in life

Cheryl — my lifelong friend since junior high school

Trudy — my dearest friend in the whole wide world

Linda — my God-given friend and confidant

Nanci McAlister, NavPress

Acknowledgments

NavPress would like to express their thanks to the many authors who have written for us and the members of the Advanced Writers and Speakers Association (AWSA), a part of Right to the Heart Ministries, and their contributions to this book about friendship. What a wonderful overview of meaningful relationships! Thank you, Linda Evans Shepherd, for catching the vision for this product. Thank you, Eva Marie Everson, for taking on a task such as this—working with over FORTY different personalities and writers to make this book take on its form and content. Thank you, Melissa Munro, for your work on the project, especially with all the details!

And a huge thank you to the creative people at NavPress: Jennifer Mahalik and Pat Miller, who made this such an attractive book to keep or give to friends.

My Invisible Friend

When I was a little girl I had an invisible friend. Her name was Charlotte, and in spite of the fact that I lived in a neighborhood with plenty of children with whom I could play — and in spite of the fact that I often did — Charlotte was my best, invisible friend.

Charlotte and I rode our bicycles together. We played with our dolls. We built imaginary homes out of the pine straw blanketing the lawn. We ate our breakfast and lunch together and, when Mother called us in for the evening meal, Charlotte sat in a chair pulled up to the table just for her and ate from an empty plate.

Of course I had real friends — a best friend even — but Charlotte was there for me twenty-four hours a day, seven days a week. She always played what I wanted to play and listened intently to my every story. Eventually I grew up, and because Charlotte never could, I took new friends into my heart. With those friendships, I have noticed that women tend to experience the dynamics of friendship in stages. Think about it. As children, we had friends we saw daily, played with daily. We typically got along okay, but sometimes we fought over toys, occasionally boys, who was "it" — silly things like that.

As we became preadolescents we spent a great deal of time pretending to be older — more grown up — than we really were. The most important issues in our lives were what we were wearing to school the next day and if we were old enough to shave our legs. We argued about which teen idol was really the cutest and prayed the darling boy in homeroom would look our way.

We became teens. We shared fashion, makeup, hairstyles,

malted milk shakes, and double dates. We argued over boys. We argued over other friends. We argued over which one of us would wear the pink gown to the prom. But by the end of that glorious evening, we were friends again. On graduation night we hugged and promised never to lose touch, but then we did.

Suddenly we were thrust into adulthood. We met new, single friends at college. Some of us married and we made new, married friends. Some of us had children and we made new, married friends with children. Just as when we were children, as we move toward our sunset years, we seek out those with whom we have much in common. Still, we hold onto those special relationships God placed in our lives when we were young and carefree, and all our free moments were spent gal-paling around.

Here in these pages we have remembered our friends—friends from early childhood, friends from adolescence, friends from young adulthood, and friends we've carried into those sunset years. This is for friends who gave birth to us and friends who we gave birth to.

This is for one of God's most precious gifts: friendship. We count it among our dearest blessings.

Eva Marie Everson, board member,
Right to the Heart Ministries

Eva Marie Everson, nine months and
Carla Tretheway, eighteen months

Make new friends, but keep the old,

one is silver and the other gold.

Traditional Camp Song

Allison Gappa Bottke and Linda Lagnada

Chitchat: *Allison was the first plus-size model ever signed by the prestigious Wilhelmina modeling agency in the early 1980s.*

Lord, Send Me a Linda!

Allison Gappa Bottke

In 1960 my family and I moved from the projects of Cleveland to the lower west side. It was there I met my first two Lindas. Linda S. and Linda B. were my very best friends. We did everything together. We grew up and parted, but their friendships were cornerstones of my life. Decades later, as a new Christian, it was another Linda B., hundreds of miles from my Ohio hometown, who befriended me and showed through her example what a woman of God was like. When I moved from that home in Arizona to Minnesota, I was leaving my Linda behind—and the pain in my heart and soul was deep. I was lonely for a heart friendship like the one I had left behind in Arizona.

"Hello, welcome to our church," a lovely woman greeted us as we entered. With a glowing smile that matched her spirit, I breathed deeply and held on to her a little tighter as we shook hands in greeting when she said, "My name is Linda. What's yours?"

Six years later, Linda L. is one of my dearest friends, and that church is our home church. God orchestrates when we open our hearts to Him.

Allison Gappa Bottke is the compiler and editor of the *God Allows U-Turns* book series.

Friends love through

all kinds of weather.

Proverbs 17:17

Kathy Shaffer and Deb Haggerty

Chitchat: One of Deb's ancestors kept the king's horses; another was hung as a horse thief.

Instant Friends, Sisters for Life

Deb Haggerty

How do you know? One minute you're meeting a stranger and the next you know you've met your "new best friend"! Kathy is such a friend. We met about two years ago in a neighborhood Bible study. I didn't really know anyone in the group and erroneously assumed that everyone else knew each other. When we finished the "coffee and chat," we gathered in the family room. Several of us sat on a sectional sofa, one on a chair at the end, while Kathy sat in a rocker across from the coffee table. Somehow, that didn't seem right — there seemed to be a separation. Patting the sofa beside me, I beckoned to Kathy, "Come, sit beside me. There's room." Smiling, she rose and joined us.

That simple gesture began a friendship more akin to having a sister. We've shared food and stories and frustrations and tears and encouragement. When one of us is shopping, we frequently check to see if the other needs something to save her the trip — and money has never changed hands. Though we sometimes disagree, we both know that this blessing of friendship God gifted us with will survive through the years.

Deb Haggerty is a noted speaker and Right to the Heart Ministries board member.

Strangers are just friends waiting to happen.

Unknown

Sally Breedlove and her friend
Jenny McDermid

From Stranger to Friend

Sally Breedlove

What is a friend? I am almost fifty and have relocated enough times in my adult life to understand and even be fairly comfortable with the process involved in cultivating relationships. And yet after every move we have made, there is always an empty time. I hope, pray, and wait, wondering if in this new place I will find even one person whose heart is open in the ways I understand. Heart connection is not an event I can produce. That's obvious. I do the prelude things and enjoy them: volunteer work with other women, a trip to a nearby town known for its hand-thrown pottery, conversations about books and children over warm mugs of latte. But all the while, I hope the other thing will begin to come into view — that moment when I begin to see a friend's heart emerging where before I saw an acquaintance's face. I stand in awe of those gift moments from God when friendship begins to form as that other woman invites me in and even while she lets me draw her out.

Sally Breedlove is the author of *Choosing Rest*.

Chitchat: Sally has been caught in a violent storm in a small boat, lost on the side of a mountain near dusk in subzero weather, and almost trapped in a flash flood in a canyon — all of which she says is easy compared to raising five kids.

I didn't find my friends …

God gave them to me.

Ralph Waldo Emerson

Left to Right: Linda Evans Shepherd,
Laura Shepherd, and Marcia Conley

Chitchat: Linda, an avid scuba diver, once dove onto a sunken
World War II battleship in the middle of the Red Sea.

Marcia — On the Job

Linda Evans Shepherd

"Laura needs twenty-four hour nursing care in your home," the doctor said. *What?* Wasn't it enough my toddler had endured a long hospitalization following a car accident? *How much more could we take?*

I looked down at my precious child, still locked in a coma, and then placed my hand on my stomach. *How am I ever going to manage Laura, the new baby, and now a house full of strangers?*

Weeks later, when Nurse Marcia walked into my home, I felt angry. I was angry at the world, at God, and especially at Marcia. *Doesn't she know this is* my *home?* But over time, I began to enjoy Marcia. We spent hours talking. Only Marcia could make me laugh; it was Marcia who listened as I talked out my grief and pain. She was there for us. When Laura finally began to come out of her coma, it was Marcia who helped me learn to live again.

Marcia worked in my home for six years before her husband took a new job two thousand miles away. I will be forever grateful for the day she walked into my house. She was God's gift to a mother with a broken heart.

Linda Evans Shepherd is an author, speaker, and founder of the Advanced Writers and Speakers Association.

Be still and know

that I am God.

Psalm 46:10, NIV

Kathy Blume and Barb Olson

Chitchat: Kathy has attended thirty-four Promise Keepers events — she loves those men things!

Be Still, My Friend

Kathy Blume

Twenty-two years ago, the bottom fell out of my life. My husband walked out, a longtime church friend died, and my dad died unexpectedly. By grace, I had a best friend who understood my pain and my needs. Barb surprised me by flying to New York to be with me. During that difficult week, she ironed my clothes, dressed my children for the funeral, made beds, and had conversations with people when I couldn't. Years earlier, Barb had been my maid of honor. My mother had separated us the night before my wedding to keep us from giggling all night. Now my mother was grateful that Barb was present to catch my tears and pray for me.

We now live only fifty miles apart. Our children are grown, we are grandmothers, and we often talk about the nursing home we will share one day. Barb lets me be quiet and reminds me that God is sovereign and attending to every detail of my life. What I have learned from our friendship is that sometimes God uses her hands to do His work.

Kathy Blume is a conference speaker and retreat leader.

A friend is someone we turn to

When our spirit needs a lift.

A friend is someone we treasure

For true friendship is a gift.

A friend is someone we laugh with

Over little personal things.

A friend is someone you're serious with

In facing whatever life brings.

A friend is someone who fills our lives

With beauty and joy and grace

And makes the world we live in

A better and happier place.

–Jean Kyler McManus–

When two of you get together on anything at all on earth and make a prayer of it, my Father in heaven goes into action. And when two or three of you are together because of me, you can be sure that I'll be there.

Matthew 18:20

Left to Right: Dianne Mathis,
Marita Littauer, and Holly Slade

The Praying Wives Club

Marita Littauer

God's Word tells us "it is bad for the person who is alone and falls, because there is no one there to help" (Ecclesiastes 4:10, NCV). I know this to be true. I have faced difficult times alone, and I have lived through them with the help of friends. Each week two friends and I get together for what we affectionately call "The Praying Wives Club." Each of us has a husband going through particularly tough times. Sworn to confidentiality, we share our burdens, lift each other up, and spend time in prayer for our spouses, our attitudes, and—most important—our marriages.

Over the past year we have seen many changes. My husband has a new job in his field. Another husband had an idea for a book that would change his career. He found a publisher for the book and got it written. The third has survived horrendous business setbacks and is now seeing the light at the end of the tunnel.

Our marriages are stronger, but not nearly as strong as our faith in God! We are "The Praying Wives Club."

Marita Littauer is the president of Class Services, Inc.

Friendship is like a fine wine;

it gets better as it gets older.

Author Unknown

Left to Right: Amanda Mellon and Laura Sabin Riley

Chitchat: Laura secretly adores extreme sports — particularly skydiving!

Blue Jean Friendship

Laura Sabin Riley

Being with Amanda is like slipping on my favorite pair of blue jeans: soft and comfortable with frayed edges and little rips. A good friendship, like a good pair of jeans, just gets better with time.

I'll never forget the first time Amanda dropped by my house. I'd been up most of the night with a sick toddler, and my house was a wreck. I was a wreck. But Amanda didn't seem to mind. She never batted an eye at the dirty dishes in the sink nor did she snicker at my scary hair, bloodshot eyes, and cough syrup-stained T-shirt. Instead, she made a comment about how comfortable my home was. Then she started doing dishes.

Together, Amanda and I have shopped, traveled, ministered, cried, laughed, prayed, played, and survived many fast-food burgers with our kids. Amanda has seen me with no makeup, flat hair, wrinkled clothes, and a bad attitude. Despite the frayed edges of my imperfection, and little rips in my temperament, Amanda doesn't pack up our friendship like some worn-out pair of pants. Instead, just like that favorite pair of jeans, the more time we spend together, the more indispensable our friendship gets.

Laura Sabin Riley is the author of
All Mothers Are Working Mothers.

Nicole Johnson and Angela Guffey

Top Ten Signs That Someone Is Your Friend

Nicole Johnson

1. They talk to you from the bathroom.
2. They fix the bald spot in the hair on the back of your head.
3. They let you take your call-waiting call if you want to.
4. They act like they've never heard your stories before.
5. They take your weapons away when you're beating yourself up.
6. They know how you like your coffee.
7. They come over to your house just to eat leftovers.
8. They find a subtle way to tell you that you have something in your teeth.
9. They keep your secrets so long they forget them.
10. They know everything about your kids and let them come over anyway.

Nicole Johnson is an actress, dramatist,
and author of *Fresh-Brewed Life.*

Chitchat: Nicole attended a dance in college and didn't realize until halfway through that she wore mismatched shoes!

A faithful friend is

an image of God.

French Proverb

Jan Coleman and Renate Sprague

Chitchat: During Jan's country-living years in the California foothills, she was known as the Pig Lady of Greenwood.

The Image of God

Jan Coleman

They say a faithful friend is the image of God. When I first met Renate, I was reeling from a rebound relationship. Unwillingly single—again—I felt like a swarm of locusts had devoured my dreams. I sought a man's arms to cushion me against more assaults of the heart. Then it was over—more pain, rejection, and regret.

Over lunch hours, Renate shared about her failed marriage, the darkness in her soul, and the promise she'd found in Isaiah 54:5-6: "Your Maker is your husband—the LORD Almighty is his name . . . The LORD will call you back as if you were a wife deserted and distressed in spirit—a wife who married young, only to be rejected (NIV)."

She said, "I dwell on this truth every day. God will never abandon or betray me. He is my mate now. He'll bring beauty out of ashes. For you, too, if you trust Him." Instead of singles groups, I hung out with Renate who gently guided me toward forgiveness and healing.

Renate's outstretched hand of friendship led me straight into the arms of another lover, the Lord Jesus, who restored my soul. He gave me a spiritual harvest that nothing can destroy.

Jan Coleman is the author of *After the Locusts*.

Tears of sadness and joy,

like dew, renew this friendship

I share with you.

And in the heart's garden,

we find the room to be ourselves,

to grow and bloom.

A blessing of beauty unsurpassed,

our friendship's a flower

that will always last.

–Author Unknown–

A hand touched me and set me trembling.

Daniel 10:10, NIV

Mindy Martens and Sharon Hoffman

Chitchat: After Sharon checked every aisle at a grocery store for her Post-it-Note list, a gentleman kindly pointed out that it was stuck to her derrière.

My Girly Gooey Friendship

Sharon Hoffman

Unwittingly, I had assumed that because Mindy and I were mother and daughter, we would not face some of the stresses I'd seen in friends' relationships. Boy, was I wrong! Though we'd both invested so much over twenty years, there was one particular holiday season when stress and tears replaced our usual camaraderie.

Shortly after an evening of harsh words, Mindy appeared in the doorway where I was drying my hands at the kitchen sink. I pressed the hand lotion pump like I always do, but this time, out popped way too much. Turning to face Mindy, I asked her if she wanted the excess lotion.

Taking my hands into hers, Mindy caressed them gently as if they were the soft fur of a kitten. We just stood there silently staring into each other's eyes, smoothing lotion into one another's hands and softening our hearts. Conflict faded away. It was as though the soothing balm of Gilead of Jeremiah 8 was being applied to our souls that day.

Now, whenever we pump out hand lotion, we always look for the nearest person to share with. This gentle gesture of love soothes selfishness into sweet softness.

Sharon Hoffman is the author of *Come Home to Comfort.*

Truly great friends are hard to find,

difficult to leave,

and impossible to forget.

G. Randolf

Left to Right: Dave Sargent, Jane Sargent,
Cynthia Spell Humbert, and David Humbert

Chitchat: Cynthia proudly owns thirty-eight Elvis albums and
has been known to sing a mean impersonation of "All Shook Up."

It's a Suthun' Thang

Cynthia Spell Humbert

The first time I heard Jane's voice, my heart smiled. Living in Kansas for almost a year, I had often felt lonely and out of place with my big hair, makeup, and Southern accent. So when I heard that familiar drawl coming out of her mouth, a kinship was formed.

God knew at that moment that He was giving me a special friend to share life's journey. Jane and I quickly began to spend countless afternoons together watching our two children play. We shared secrets, hopes, prayers, tears, and laughter. I wasn't lonely anymore.

My heart broke when she told me she and her family would be moving. Five years later, we have learned that distance may keep us from seeing each other, but our friendship can remain constant. True commitment to encourage each other means that even when we may not speak for a while, we don't get our feelings hurt; we just pick right back up where we left off. When we need each other, we are only a phone call away.

Her faithful friendship reminds me that even when we sometimes feel far away from Jesus, He is always waiting to hear from us, and our connection to Him is never broken.

Cynthia Spell Humbert is the author of
Deceived by Shame, Desired by God.

The greatest good you can do for another

is not just to share your riches,

but to reveal to him his own.

Benjamin Disraeli

Marie
Nemec

Carmen
Leal

Chitchat: In the peace corps in Mali, Carmen learned French
and the local language, Bambara, and ate "don't ask, don't tell"
cuisine such as rat, cat, cock's comb, and fish eyes.

Cyber-Friend

Carmen Leal

In January 1998, my thirty-six-year-old brother, Merrill, died of a rare liver disease called primary sclerosing cholangitis. At the time, I was caring for my husband, who was in the middle stages of Huntington's disease. With little income and increasing medical bills, I somehow scraped together enough money to fly from Orlando to Kansas City for a few special days with Merrill, my parents, and other siblings.

Two days after I returned home, Merrill passed away. I sent an e-mail to an on-line Christian writers group asking for prayer and a way for my two sons and me to attend the funeral. Less than an hour later my on-line friend Marie, a member of the group, sent me an amazing e-mail. She offered to give me her complete paycheck to help pay for the three tickets. Marie worked full-time, not because she needed the income, but for what the money could do to help others in need.

Marie and I have met face-to-face several times since 1998 and I'm honored to call her my friend. Thanks to her generosity I was able to celebrate my brother's life with the rest of my family.

Carmen Leal is the author of *WriterSpeaker.com*.

You've touched my heart.

Ruth 2:13

Ken Rada Photography, Atlanta

Eva Marie Everson and Robi Lipscomb

Chitchat: By invitation, Eva danced in front of the parliament building in Nassau, Bahamas.

In the Face of Tragedy

Eva Marie Everson

September 11, 2001, is a date we remember well; it falls into the file of "Where were you when Kennedy was assassinated?" Years from now our children and grandchildren will ask, "Where were you when the towers fell?"

My answer will be, "In New York City . . . in the heart of Manhattan . . . trying desperately to contact family and friends by phone to tell them we're alive."

My husband and I tried for hours to reach the outside world, but the lines were either on overload or shut down. Still, using our cell phone, we made continuous efforts to dial out. Finally, a little after two o'clock, the lines opened and for the first time we were able to speak to our children. When I checked our voice mail, I discovered nearly thirty calls from friends, begging us to call, sobbing, praying *Please be okay!*

Not one call touched me more than any other; they all brought comfort and reminders of our connection. One such message came from my best friend, Robi: "Hello? This is your best friend . . . I love you . . . I don't say it enough, but I do . . . please be okay. *Please?*" Best friends tell you they love you— when you need it most.

Eva Marie Everson is the author of
Summon the Shadows, a novel.

Laugh and the world laughs with you.

Cry and you cry with your girlfriends.

Laurie Kuslansky

Donald A. Scott Photography

Left to Right: Linda Aleahmad,
Mary Scott, and Martha Bolton

Chitchat: Martha once cooked a smoked turkey for seventeen hours. She doesn't recommend it.

Friends Forever, and That's No Foolin'

Martha Bolton

We met through the National League of American Pen Women. Linda Aleahmad, Mary Scott, Margaret Brownley, and I were barely published, raising families, and trying our best to balance the pursuit of a full-time writing career with full-time family life. We became such good friends that we made a pact to meet at a prearranged restaurant each April 1.

When we made our pledge, we didn't realize how much life we would share together—good and bad. Between the four of us we've celebrated hundreds of published books, poetry, and articles, as well as awards, honors, a master's degree, a marriage and family therapist license, children's marriages, births of grandchildren, and much more. We've also seen our public accomplishments arrive simultaneously with painful private experiences. We've faced financial challenges, the loss of a child, two husbands' heart attacks, one divorce, deaths of parents and siblings, and a cancer battle.

We've been there for each other through it all. Ours is a friendship built on laughter, a love for words, faith in each other and in God. April 1, a day to celebrate enduring friendship? You'd better believe it . . . and that's no foolin'!

Martha Bolton was a staff writer for Bob Hope
for over fifteen years.

To live in prayer together

is to walk in love together.

Margaret Moore Jacobs

Left to right: Katie Godfrey, Dale Lipscomb,
Robi Lipscomb, Christian Godfrey, and J. R. Godfrey

Chitchat: *Robi's real name is Robilene, using the first part of
her dad's name (Robert) and the last part of her mom's name
(Paulene) with an "i" in the middle.*

Living the Promise

Robi Lipscomb

Good friends often share many life experiences—including pain and heartbreak. Katie and I have been friends since college. As the years passed, the miles grew between us but the friendship stayed strong. One day, she called to say something was wrong with her first son. Instead of reaching childhood milestones like walking and feeding himself, he had begun to digress. J.R. was diagnosed with Batten,* a terminal disease with no known treatment. A few years later, I called Katie when my oldest son was diagnosed with Type 1 diabetes. She was the one person who understood what I was going through, from the depression to insurance paperwork frustrations. Finally, a call from Katie told me J.R.'s five-year life, full of struggles and moments of joy, had ended. Days later, we shared the funeral of her child, one of the deepest moments in a friendship.

Afterward, as Katie thanked me for being there, I said, "You're welcome, but I hope you never return the favor."

"You know I would be there for you through anything," she replied. And that's what real friendship is: living "I will be there for you through anything."

Robi Lipscomb is the author of *The Stewardship Safari.*

---

*For more information on Batten: http://www.bdsra.org/index.htm

There's an opportune time to do things,

a right time for everything on the earth:

A right time to cry and another to laugh.

Ecclesiastes 3:1,4

Mona Gansberg Hodgson and Shirley Millar

An Off-Season Friend

Mona Gansberg Hodgson

We've all had friends who, when put to the test of the various seasons mentioned in the third chapter of Ecclesiastes, proved to be fair-weather friends. Some friendships thrive in times of ease and celebration, but wane during seasons of pain and grief. Ten years ago Shirley Millar gave me the gift of an off-season friendship.

When my dad was diagnosed with cancer and died five months later, Shirley walked with me. In a time when the masses backed away altogether or felt a need to fill the emotional gap with words—usually platitudes—she gave quiet solace. And though she was poised to listen, she wasn't intimidated by the silence when I couldn't speak. She offered the encompassing comfort of a hug and a quiet permission to cry when tears tugged at my eyelids.

Modeling the all-season friendship we have with Jesus, Shirley showed me that a true friend walks with you through the off-seasons as well as through the peak seasons.

Mona Gansberg Hodgson is the author
of the I Wonder picture book series.

Chitchat: *The corner of Mona's office contains a set of conga drums.*

Deeds, and not fine speeches,

are the proof of love.

Spanish Proverb

Laura Jensen Walker and Lana Yarbrough

Chitchat: Laura joined the Air Force after high school and "flew a typewriter" (as a clerk typist) across Europe for Uncle Sam for the next five years.

Unconditional Love

Laura Jensen Walker

Lana wrote the manual on being a best friend. A few days after my mastectomy, I wasn't quite at my movie-star best. My hair was greasy; I hadn't had a bath or shower in the three days since my surgery. I was lopsided and I had a disgusting, plastic, football-shaped drainage tube under my arm filling up with icky bodily fluids. Ugh.

That's when Lana came over to visit and cheer me up. She gently hugged me, then wrinkled her petite little nose and said, "Laura, you stink. We need to give you a bath."

"I love you, too."

Now, Lana's five-foot-two and maybe 105 pounds; I'm five-foot-seven and haven't seen 105 since junior high. Plus, I was still pretty sore from the surgery and not moving very easily.

But Lana boosted me up from the couch and supported me down the hall into the bathroom. She gently helped me undress and ease into a nice warm bath. As she shampooed my hair I said, "Lana, maybe you should give up teaching and become a nurse instead."

"No way," she replied. "I wouldn't do this for anybody else."

Laura Jensen Walker is the author of
Mental-Pause . . . and Other Midlife Laughs.

A version of this story originally appeared in *Thanks for the Mammogram* (Fleming H. Revell, 2000).

A friend is someone who knows the song in your heart
and can sing it back to you when you have
forgotten the words.

Unknown

Lynn Morrissey, Sheridan, and
Fern Morrissey

Chitchat: Lynn's college years included a vocal ensemble
performance in the White House Ballroom with Pat and Tricia
Nixon in attendance.

Mother's Melody

Lynn D. Morrissey

Grandmother was fond of telling me to treat my mother like a queen because "a mother is a girl's best friend." While I have always adored my mother, I never fully understood Grandmother's wisdom until I became a mother. To honor my mother I read this poem at a tea where she was in attendance. There was not a dry eye in the place.

Mother's Melody
She sang to me unconditionally as I grew in her secret cocoon
and bloomed to completion.
She sang contentment. Nesting me at her breast,
we rocked and rocked in quilted quiet.
My curls rose and fell with her breath.
She sang ivory lullabies, rock-a-bye babies,
hush-a-byes, by yon bonnie banks and farmers' dells.
The tunes soared and swelled 'til I was compelled
to sing-a-ring around her rosy beauty.
She sang comfort on rain-throated days and
brought tea and toast.
I floated in her blue-quilt sea, gently bedded.
She sang love to me sacrificially.
I was in her. Now she's in me. I am my mother's melody.

Unlike any other friend, one's mother makes the ultimate sacrifice—surrendering her body to give birth and sacrificing desires in order to raise her child to adulthood.

Lynn D. Morrissey is the author of
best-selling *Seasons of a Woman's Heart*.

Stoop down and reach out to those who are oppressed.

Share their burdens, and so complete Christ's law.

Galatians 6:2

Kathe
Wunnenburg

Carol
Kent

Becky
Freeman

Chitchat: Years ago Carol was driving her 1959 Pontiac and the accelerator stuck. She hit four cars, a fire hydrant, a park bench, and the front window of a building before realizing she could have stopped the car by turning off the engine.

Extravagant Love

Carol Kent

It had been a devastating year; my son had been arrested for a serious crime and my dreams for his future had evaporated all hope. My husband and I gathered our liquid assets for the down payment of an expensive criminal defense attorney.

Nine months into this ordeal, my friend Becky suggested she'd like to organize a group of friends to support our family. Another close friend, Kathe, e-mailed that the Lord was nudging her in the same direction. These friends launched a monthly prayer letter that gave our extended network of family and friends updates on how to pray specifically for our needs. Our family became the recipient of the most lavish love imaginable. Our mailbox was brimming with cards of encouragement; flowers and gifts arrived on our doorstep.

Becky and I began praying for each other's family needs and a sisterlike bond developed as we shared our disappointments. We discovered what it means to carry each other's burdens and fulfill the law of Christ. Kathe called or e-mailed at unexpected times—always when my heart needed a lift. My devastating year became the year God taught me the meaning of true compassion through the extravagant love of friends.

Carol Kent is the president of Speak Up Speaker Services.

Friends are God's way of taking care of us.

Unknown

Left to Right: Rosemary O'Day,
Dolley Carlson, and Mary Cushing

Chitchat: Dolley plays the red-haired grandmother in the
Pillsbury Crescent Roll television commercial.

God's On Your Side

We were both young women working in Boston when I met my friend Rosemary O'Day. At the time I was estranged from God and, although I smiled easily, my heart was broken. Then God lovingly sent this "angel-friend" to gently lead me back to Him.

When I was a teenager my family appeared to be perfect, but there was so much pain in our home. My parents drank "socially" until deep disappointments came into their lives. Then drinking became a way of life—every day, every night, and often into the early morning—bringing upheaval and violence. After five years of living like this, my mother died; she was thirty-seven and I was seventeen. It was the day I turned my back on God.

Week after week Rosemary would invite me to church. My answer was always, "No, thank you." One day she followed her invitation with four little words that carried me straight into the arms of my heavenly Father: "God's on your side." That was over twenty-five years ago. We now live three thousand miles apart, yet our friendship has never waned over time, distance, or absence. I call her my "angel-friend" because of her heavenly ways.

Dolley Carlson is the author of the Gifts From The Heart series.

Friendship is one mind

in two bodies.

Mencius

Darcy Miller Turner and
Kathy Collard Miller

Next Year, I Pay!

Kathy Collard Miller

My grown daughter, Darcy, and I are great friends. We recently did something new: we went away to a hotel spa. Other than mother-daughter retreats when she was younger, we've never spent a weekend together alone and I was thrilled that she invited me to come with her. It was her way of saying, "Thank you for helping with my wedding."

We had a fabulous time! We had a facial, herbal body wrap, and back massage. We went shopping at antique stores and an outlet mall. We ate and played Scrabble and ate and drove around seeing the sights and ate and golfed and ate . . .

I'm blessed to have a friend like my daughter who respects her mom and wants to spend time with her. We hope to make this event an annual one. Next year, I pay!

Kathy Collard Miller is a beloved women's retreat speaker.

Chitchat: Kathy had her first short-term missionary trip in 1969, and took her most recent one to Indonesia, where she spoke eight times in a week to Christians eager to learn.

But the wisdom that comes from heaven is first of all pure;
then peace-loving, considerate, submissive, full of mercy
and good fruit, impartial and sincere.

James 3:17, NIV

Marlene Bagnull

Mary Tyson

Chitchat: As a teenager, Marlene felt called to be a
missionary — never imagining that God meant a "literary"
missionary, especially since she hated English in high school.

Telephone Buddy

Marlene Bagnull

We never did the typical girlfriend things together. By the time we became close friends, Mary was pretty much homebound except for visits to her doctor. Her telephone became her lifeline—and mine. How many times I called her needing to talk! Mary instinctively knew how long to allow me for venting and when to cut me off before I dug an even deeper hole.

By example, Mary taught me the principles of wisdom in James 3:17. She was always "straightforward and sincere" and full of "mercy and good deeds." When my husband was out of work, I have no doubt she was the source of many of the anonymous gifts our pastor handed us. And when my stepfather died and I assumed the responsibility of caring for my mother, who had a condition similar to Alzheimer's, Mary became the mother Mom could no longer be.

Both Mary and my mother are now with the Lord. Mary is no longer limited by bones that break, or my mother by a mind that doesn't work. One day I will see them again. Until then—especially when the phone rings—I'm reminded of Mary.

Marlene Bagnull's latest work is *My Turn to Care—Encouragement for Caregivers of Aging Parents.*

There's a Miracle Called Friendship

There's a miracle called friendship

That dwells in the heart

You don't know how it happens

Or when it gets to start

But you know the special lift

It always brings

And you realize that friendship

Is God's most precious gift!

–Author Unknown–

There are spaces between our fingers
so that another person's fingers can fill them in.

Unknown

Karen O'Connor

Chitchat: Karen hiked to the top of Mount Whitney at the age of fifty-seven!

Friendship Tea

Karen O'Connor

I looked around my new house the day after we moved in, then sat down and cried! I missed our old neighborhood, the park down the street, my kids' school. I wondered if I'd ever feel at home in this new community where I didn't know another soul. "Lord, help me get a grip," I prayed.

Within moments I noticed a woman about my age walking up the driveway. I dabbed my eyes with a tissue, tucked in my shirt, and opened the door.

"Hello," the woman said. "I'm Jean Sanchez. I live in the yellow house at the end of the cul-de-sac. Welcome to our neighborhood." Then she handed me a lovely glass jar encircled with a bright red bow. A pretty handwritten label across the front read *Friendship Tea.* "I look forward to getting to know you. I hope we can be friends."

Tears welled in my eyes again—but this time from gratitude. Here was a gift of friendship so lovely, so unexpected, so like the Lord that I was speechless! I reached out and hugged Jean, my new neighbor—and new friend—thanked her, and then invited her in to share a cup of friendship tea.

Karen O'Connor is the author of
Basket of Blessings: 31 Days to a More Grateful Heart.

It's so much friendlier with two.

Winnie the Pooh

Kirkie
Morrissey

. . . and one
of her hiking
friends, Ann
Brosh

Chitchat: Kirkie was a professional child model whom a
Chicago newspaper heralded as "the new Shirley Temple."

Let's Take a Hike!

Kirkie Morrissey

One of my favorite things to do is to tell a friend to "take a hike"—and then go with her! Walking is one of my favorite ways of spending time with a friend. It's so easy to walk and talk—less threatening than an eyeball-to-eyeball conversation that can make you feel "on the spot." The beauty of nature, love of friendship, and relaxed circumstance seem to provide just the right atmosphere for intimate sharing.

I enjoy this with casual or treasured friends. Last week when walking with my friend Cindy, we found ourselves sharing some painful experiences from the past. As we spoke of our heartaches, we also shared how the Lord had helped us in those times.

We would stop to rest and just be quiet together, soaking up the sunshine and enjoying the magnificent panorama of the Rocky Mountains before us. We sensed God's presence. By the time we returned to her home we were refreshed and our hearts had been knit closer together.

When I'm with my close friend Ann, it seems like I can more easily vent the "pent-up" frustrations as we walk. Problems and heart issues that need to be worked through are dealt with as we walk and talk. Not only is it good for the body, it's good for the soul!

Kirkie Morrissey is the author of *At Jesus' Feet.*

My Champion, my Friend,

while I'm weeping my eyes out before God.

I appeal to the One who represents mortals before God

as a neighbor stands up for a neighbor.

Job 16:20-21

Cristine Bolley

Marrie Porter and
friend Claire Smith

Chitchat: Cris and her husband, Jim, collect Model-T Fords and
drive them in parades and on tours.

Chocolate Kisses

Cristine Bolley

Marrie was among the oldest members of the church, always faithful to remind us that she'd been praying for us. Even years after I moved away, she continued to call, asking about my girls. Her calls always came in the midst of some new calamity and her beautiful southern accent always calmed me down.

Marrie was ninety-one when she stepped into heaven. The week before, she took her weekly meals to shut-ins and bowled with her ladies league. At her memorial service, one of her grandsons (her entire family serves the Lord!) told us about Marrie's prayer book found beside her favorite chair. In the prayer book were the names of the people for whom she prayed every day. Her family used to tease her for falling asleep in that chair, but she always denied it, saying she was praying.

Marrie grew up in the South where she picked cotton and believed that wealth meant having a chocolate bar every day. At her funeral, her grandchildren handed out Hershey's Kisses. Once home, I cried over the loss of my friend. Then I made a prayer book to put beside my favorite chair and unwrapped the chocolate Kiss she'd left for me.

Cristine Bolley is the author of *A Gift from Saint Nicholas.*

Life is a garden,

Good friends are the flowers.

And time spent together …

Life's happiest hours

And friendships like flowers,

bloom ever more fair …

when carefully tended by dear friends who care.

–Helen Steiner Rice–

Ken Rada Photography, Atlanta

Marita Littauer and Georgia Shaffer

Glorious Day — Georgia's Story

Georgia Shaffer

"I can't make it happen," I told my best friend, Marita Littauer.

"Don't worry," she said. "I'll take care of it."

And with the following invitation, she did.

It is a Glorious Day!

Georgia Turns Fifty!

Ten years ago, my friends and I turned forty. As they celebrated their big day, I prepared for a bone marrow transplant. It saddened me that I wouldn't have a party that year, but even more so was the ever-present knowledge that I may not even live. I resolved that if I lived to see fifty, I'd have a large garden party.

I shared this with Marita—feeling sad that after all these years I still didn't have the energy to host such an event. Marita took matters into her own hands. She flew from New Mexico to my home in Pennsylvania to help me celebrate more than my birthday; she helped me celebrate my life. She coordinated and catered the party, inviting those closest to me.

The party turned out far more splendid than anything I'd dreamed possible. That evening, I thanked God for my health and for Marita, who not only brightened my life, but also made turning fifty simply glorious.

Georgia Shaffer is the author of *A Gift of Mourning Glories*.

Chitchat: Georgia's great-great-grandfather and his six brothers founded the community she lives in.

Glorious Day — Marita's Story

Marita Littauer

A while ago I conducted an e-mail survey when I needed some examples on "expectations" for a speech I was preparing. I had to laugh when one of the responses came back, "I expect my friend to keep me company when I do dishes." While I'd never articulated it, that was one of *my* expectations. I have a headset telephone and as I do mundane tasks, I call my buddy Georgia, who lives on the other side of the country. She is also the first person I call when I have some great news to share, when I just want to yak, or when I am in tears.

When I had the opportunity to do something special for her, there was no question that I would do whatever it took. Having almost lost her life to cancer ten years earlier, she needed a party to celebrate her fiftieth birthday. I rejoice in her life and I love to throw a party. After flying across the country, cooking the food, and serving her guests, the party-goers asked if my services were for hire. My answer was no; my gift was bought with love and my services were not for hire.

Marita Littauer is the president of Class Services, Inc.

Chitchat: Marita began riding motorcycles thirty years ago; she still holds her motorcycle license and owns a classic dirt bike.

Strip down, start running—and never quit!

No extra spiritual fat, no parasitic sins.

Keep your eyes on Jesus,

who both began and finished this race we're in.

Hebrews 12:1-2

Left to Right: Jan Frank, Ginny Lukei, and
Marian McFadden

Chitchat: Jan's fortieth birthday lasted forty-eight hours
because she was in transit from Singapore to the United States.

On the "Fast-Track"

Jan Frank

Years ago, Ginny, Marian, and I embarked on a journey that began with my suggestion: "Why don't we jot down the three most important prayer needs in our lives and then we can set a time to fast and pray for one another?" We sat prayerfully for a few moments, then each wrote three brief requests on Post-it Notes and pulled out our calendars. We mapped out a rotation of fasting and prayer, and committed to pray daily. One of us would fast each day for the following ten days and then we would meet back together to share what God had done.

We learned many things during that fast. One of the most significant was that God was changing our hearts. The requests that weighed so heavily became secondary to what God was working in us. We saw God's hand moving in our hearts and lives, sometimes in opposite ways to what we would have imagined. We encouraged and lifted each other, as we could see more clearly what God was doing in one another than we could see what He was doing in us individually.

Praying on the "fast-track" continues, and together we're feasting on God's faithfulness.

Jan Frank is the author of *Door of Hope*.

Love talked about can be easily turned aside but love demonstrated is irresistible.

W. Stanley Mooneyham

Patty LaRoche and Lindsey O' Connor

Chitchat: Lael has actually been down a manhole (and popped back out with a campaign sign for a TV ad).

Pajama Party

Lael Arrington

I'm a conference/convention junkie. Just put me in a room with a view and a girlfriend or two, popping pillow mints, spilling our secrets, throwing ideas like spaghetti on the walls—seeing what sticks.

A thousand miles from home, a convention pajama party is interrupted. Throughout the next day, mother-to-be Lindsey sinks a little lower in her chair. Her bleeding will not stop. In a downtown hospital, Patty and I wait. Two silk-suited aliens in a too-bright emergency room too far from home for anyone to come in time.

After the examination, Patty and I hover near Lindsey's bed. "She's losing her baby."

Lindsey leans on me for the support our years of friendship afford. To make it down the hall, she leans on Patty's strong arms because mine are weak from rheumatoid arthritis. She's just met Patty.

In a Kingdom moment we have the honor of being Jesus to Lindsey. Jesus praying, Jesus mourning. Jesus presenting her the half-dead flowers from someone's desk, coaxing a morphine smile. Jesus smoothing her hair and walking beside her wheelchair to the sonogram that searches her womb and finds . . . nothing. Jesus wrapping her in our arms with we-can't-do-anything-else love.

God provides for a friend's every need.

Lael Arrington is a speaker and the author
of *Pilgrim's Progress Today*.

A true friend knows your weaknesses
but shows you your strengths;
feels your fears but fortifies your faith;
sees your anxieties but frees your spirit;
recognizes your disabilities but emphasizes your possibilities.

William Arthur Ward

Paula Rinehart and Jennifer Ennis

Hot Coffee, Whining Children, and Godiva Chocolate

Paula Rinehart

To me, a real friend means having a shared history. Of all the things I value about a close friend, it's this mental scrapbook of memories that matters the most—the endless cups of coffee and conversation, the camping trip with a tent full of whining children in the rain, the tears and the laughter that ease some dark days. It adds up over time—like one pearl strung together with the next and the next until you realize that you actually have something here of real value. I know how tempting it is to quietly toss away a friendship when things get tough. But then I think of all the history and all the memories, and I listen again to the Bible's wisdom to "bear with" each other. The rewards so outweigh the costs. A good friendship, full of memories that span the years, is like carrying around my own secret stash of Godiva chocolate that I get to savor quietly anytime I want.

Paula Rinehart is the author of *Strong Women, Soft Hearts*.

Chitchat: Paula grew up in a house that her father built right after World War II and her bedroom window overlooked the Blue Ridge Mountains.

Some people come into our lives and quickly go.

Some stay for a while and leave footprints on our hearts ...

and we are never the same.

Unknown

Silvia Shoultz and Judy Hampton

Jesus and Ham Sandwiches

Judy Hampton

We all know that God created women to be quite different from men, one of the biggest differences being that women love to talk. They also love to do lunch. My favorite thing to do with a friend is to have lunch together. Head to a restaurant on any given weekday at lunchtime, and you'll see more women having lunch together than ducks swimming in a pond. The restaurant sounds like a henhouse. Why? Women need friends. Women need to share their deepest feelings. Talking things out diminishes the pain. And sharing joy with a girlfriend is like getting three scoops of ice cream for a dime.

I remember a special lunch shared with a new friend. She is Jewish. During our lunch, I began to share the gospel with her. She hung on my every word. She asked all the questions we dream of being asked by a nonbeliever and I listened ever so intently. A few months later she invited Jesus Christ into her heart and received Him as her Savior. These days, when we meet for lunch, we are free to talk about Jesus . . . over ham sandwiches.

Judy Hampton is a speaker and the author of
Under the Circumstances.

Chitchat: As a preteen, Judy drank supplements to put on weight. (Now she prays for help to lose it!)

A genuine friendship is a heavenly present.

It blesses our hearts because God's love is in it.

Evelyn McCurdy

Lorraine Pintus and Linda Dillow

Garments of Friendship

Linda Dillow

A friend is clothed with Seraphim wings,
running ahead of me shouting,
"Holy, Holy, Holy," pushing me into the
Presence of God.

The spirit of Aaron and Hur clothe a friend.
Running behind me, she sits me on a rock, holds up
my weary hands, and waits with me in silence
while the Lord fights my battle.

Encouragement clothes a friend.
Like the Holy Spirit, she runs beside me, and
whispers, "Grow in your God-given gifts."

The love of Jesus clothes a friend.
Running into my heart, she speaks the truth
in love, even when it hurts.

Linda Dillow is the author of *Calm My Anxious Heart*.

Chitchat: Linda regularly accepts speaking engagements on the
East and West Coasts so she can see her grandchildren.

A friend is someone with whom I may be sincere.

Before [her], I may think aloud.

Ralph Waldo Emerson

Theresa Cain and Leslie Vernick

Chitchat: Leslie's claim to fame is winning second place in her annual elementary jump rope competition.

My Soul Sister

Leslie Vernick

Have you ever prayed for a special friend—a kindred spirit, someone who would know you inside and out and love you just the same? I've always longed for a relationship with a girlfriend like the friendship between Jonathan and David.

God answered my prayer. Theresa and I began to develop a very special bond. We met in a Sunday school class over fifteen years ago and I was immediately drawn to her. Theresa's deep, dark eyes revealed a mixture of passion and pain, but it wasn't just her eyes that captured me. It was her heart. Throughout the class she spoke of God in such an intimate way it made my insides ache for more of Him. I love Theresa not only because we have great fun shopping, eating, and gabbing, but because she isn't afraid to ask hard questions and challenge me in my walk with God. "How's your quiet time going?" she probes over plenty of giggles, chocolate, and tea. "Is Jesus speaking to your heart lately? What specifically can I pray about for you this week?" And, as only a true friend would, she invites me to do the same for her.

Leslie Vernick is the author of
How to Act Right When Your Spouse Acts Wrong.

If you live to be a hundred,

I want to live to be a hundred minus one day,

so I never have to live without you.

Winnie the Pooh

Shirley Dahlquist and Kendra Smiley

Fellowship Postponed

Kendra Smiley

My friend Shirley discovered she had breast cancer. Her physician did a radical mastectomy and deemed her prognosis poor. Nevertheless, Shirley successfully fought the dreaded, life-threatening disease for years after that initial diagnosis. She was an inspiration!

After eight years, her cancer returned with a vengeance and she entered a hospice program near her home and far from mine. I called her every week. Some days our conversations were lively and fun, and other days she was too tired or sick to enjoy conversing. On those days I reminded her I loved her and would call next week.

Ultimately, I planned a trip to see her. I booked the flight and planned to arrive and go straight to her bedside. As I drove to the airport, my car phone rang. It was Shirley's husband. Shirley had died just an hour before. Now our visit was impossible. I had missed my window of opportunity.

After many tears were shed, I suddenly and joyfully realized our visit had not been canceled—it had merely been postponed.

Kendra Smiley is the author of *High-Wire Mom*.

Hold a true friend with both hands.

Nigerian Proverb

Charlotte Adelsperger and Marit Devold

Chitchat: As a teen, Charlotte led her softball team to five consecutive championships with her fast pitch.

Across the Ocean

Marit and I met on a ship on the Atlantic Ocean—forty-one years ago! I was a teacher returning from summer studies in Norway. Marit, a Norwegian student, was headed for a college not far from my home in Missouri. It was the beginning of an enduring friendship that grew over the years in spite of the ocean between us.

While Marit was here we enjoyed evenings together sharing our faith, our dreams, and prayers for the future. Marit's dream of becoming a teacher became reality and after her return to Norway, we wrote often.

Years later, in 1998, my husband, Bob, and I traveled to Norway. What incredible joy when Marit and I hugged each other after thirty-seven years! That evening she showed me a scrapbook in which she had pasted all the letters and pictures I had ever sent. I was so touched.

More recently, Marit and her husband Ivar came to visit us. These personal visits strengthened an already special friendship as we reminisced about the past and recalled the goodness of the Lord. Marit sent a Scripture to me years ago: "And my God will meet all your needs according to his glorious riches in Christ Jesus" (Philippians 4:19, NIV). God has, indeed, blessed our friendship and given us many opportunities to meet each other's personal needs—even though we live an ocean apart.

Charlotte Adelsperger is a speaker and coauthor of
Through the Generations.

Gently encourage the stragglers,

and reach out for the exhausted,

pulling them to their feet.

1 Thessalonians 5:11

Left to Right: Charlene Ann Baumbich, Marry
Kauffold, Nancy Stetson, Donna M. Chavez

Chitchat: Charlene was a 1996 Celebrity Judge for White Castle
Hamburgers' Fifth Annual Cravetime Recipe Contest.

Creative Encouragements

Charlene Ann Baumbich

Years ago, in the aftermath of yet another Secretaries' Day, I bemoaned the pathetic fact that when one works for herself in her own messy home office, nobody shows up with candy or flowers to applaud her clerical prowess. Another holiday bites the lonesome, working woman's dust. Later that year, I had to listen to working friends blather on about their upcoming office Christmas parties! *Sigh.* The more I got to grumbling within myself, the more miserable I became until I finally yanked the phone to my face to vent aloud to another freelancer friend. "Blah, blah, whine, whine," went our highly relatable conversation.

The God-light dawned in our hearts when we hit on the idea of recognizing one another, and thus launched our first Nonoffice Christmas Party! We invited a couple other freelance workers, met at a restaurant, brought gifts, and patted ourselves and each other on the back for relentlessly pursuing our dreams and goals. Years later, our annual event is now scheduled weeks in advance and our small but mighty group also enjoys occasional nonoffice gatherings, just to exchange energies. What a good idea for us nonoffice girlfriends!

Charlene Ann Baumbich is a national speaker and author.

My father always used to say that when you die,

if you've got five real friends,

then you've had a great life.

Lee Iacocca

Left to Right: Robin Holland, Vickey Banks, Mary Ann
Grisham, Jeanette Johnson, and Kelley Green

Chitchat: Vickey won the Miss Poise and Appearance title in
the Oklahoma Junior Miss Pageant the same year her senior class
nominated her "Biggest Klutz."

Getting Together

Vickey Banks

Getting together used to be so easy. Once a month the five of us would grab the craft we were working on, kiss our hubbies good-bye, and thoroughly enjoy an unrushed evening of girl time.

Fast-forward almost twenty years and our lives couldn't look more different. We live in four separate cities, have fifteen children between us, don't have time for crafts, and would consider an evening of unrushed girl time a miracle of spectacular proportions! And yet, once a year we attempt the impossible: getting together for a weekend of celebrating our friendship. Getting there is never easy.

Just after our last trip, four of us received one of those dreaded middle-of-the-night phone calls. Robin was having a brain aneurysm. *Would we ever all get together again?* I wondered as I raced to her hometown hospital. Suddenly, it hit me. Of course we would! As Christians, we know we will enjoy eternity together in heaven.

Robin made it through surgery and I thanked God for that. But I also drove home dreaming of the day we would all be together in heaven. The road to get there may not always be easy, but the celebration will be worth it!

Vickey Banks is the author of *Sharing His Secrets*.

We are each of us angels with only one wing

and can only fly embracing each other.

Luciano de Crescenzo

Betty Southard and Ann Plas

Chitchat: Betty modeled for a weekly fashion show at a restaurant near Arizona State University for ten years — as the only model.

In the Image of Christ

Betty Southard

A trusted leader in ministry had betrayed me. After honestly pouring out my thoughts and feelings to this person, I inadvertently overheard her sharing what I had said to another. It was obvious this was not the first time they had discussed me. They were negating all I had said. I was devastated! My heart was broken. I felt humiliated and then angry.

My dear friend Ann, seeing the look on my face, asked, "What's wrong?" After telling her what happened, she did the very best thing a friend could do; she held me and let me cry. She didn't try to fix the situation. She didn't preach to me. She just listened and loved—never condoning or condemning, just being there, understanding, and loving. She modeled Christ's response to our hurts, trials, and grief.

In time I was able to speak to both women and let them know I had heard, express my disappointment and hurt, and forgive. Our relationships have been restored, but it was Ann's love that made it possible to process the pain and rely on God's promises. What a friend!

Betty Southard is the author of *The Mentoring Quest*.

Just like a rose,

so precious and rare,

is the forever friendship

the two of us share.

Planted with kindness,

It's warmed by the sun

of caring and sharing,

laughter and fun.

It's grounded in trust

and nurtured by love,

with a sprinkling of grace

from God up above.

–Author Unknown–

With a friend you can face the worst.

Ecclesiastes 4:12

Fran Caffey Sandin and Linda Gilbert

Chitchat: Fran won the Texas "Betty Crocker Homemaker of Tomorrow" contest, which provided a scholarship that allowed her to pursue her dream of being a nurse.

Nickel Advice

Fran Caffey Sandin

Linda and I have a standing joke. When one of us calls in distress, we hang out a homemade sign on the front door: *Psychiatric Help — 5 cents* (like Lucy in *Peanuts*). Usually, we just need a listening ear and a cup of hot tea.

Our lasting friendship began as nursing students. Eventually we settled in the same community, attended the same church, and lived in similar houses only a few blocks apart. Through the years we have encouraged each other with Scripture, laughed together, and shared confidential concerns about our families. Linda listens, sifts through, and forgets most of it except the issue that needs specific prayer. Then she prays for me and my burden is lifted. Mutual confidence and trust has sealed our friendship.

She was with me when our youngest son was born and again seventeen months later when he died. We are connected heart to heart through our love for the Lord and each other. Linda has been my greatest cheerleader. Ours is a treasured friendship, a common bond that money cannot buy. She will be moving soon and I gave her a decorative pillow that says, "Friendship travels everywhere."

Fran Caffey Sandin is the author of
Touching the Clouds.

A true friend unbosoms freely, advises justly, assists readily,

adventures boldly, takes all patiently, defends courageously,

and continues a friend unchangeably.

William Penn

Mary J. Gerlinger and Helene Ashker

Chitchat: Helene's mother was born in the same town as Jesus.

She Knows Me Well

Helene Ashker

My friendship with Mary started over thirty-five years ago when I was in Denver on my first ministry assignment with The Navigators. Since then we have vacationed together—trips that took us to Puerto Vallarta and the beaches of Oregon. For fun we ride bikes, take walks along the beach, entertain other friends, and compete with board games.

What makes our relationship special is the freedom we feel to agree or disagree when we discuss problems and political issues, or when sharing our hearts. What has been most valuable is our ability to express how we feel about an issue, trusting the other to listen, respond, and affirm with respect. Most of all I appreciate our mutual, loyal love for the Lord and each other.

When I moved back to Denver after being away for seventeen years, I was lonelier than I anticipated. I called her more frequently than usual (we have always lived in different states) and it was always good to hear her voice. She commented that she knew I had adjusted to the change when I didn't call as often. She knows me well.

Helene Ashker is the author of *Jesus Changes Women*.

Wounds from a friend can be trusted.

Proverbs 27:6, NIV

Becky Freeman

Gracie Malone

Chitchat: Becky gave birth to all four of her children at home — in natural, cozy, excruciating pain.

Analyze This Friendship

Becky Freeman

Gracie Malone is one of the rarest of friends: the sort I unburden my deepest soul to one minute, then find myself engaging in sitcom-like dialogue the next. Take yesterday's lunchtime conversation, for example.

"I am reading this book, Gracie," I said as we nestled into the restaurant booth. "It's about how all of our pain results from childhood wounds. But I think my wound must be somewhere after childhood because almost all of my childhood memories are good."

"Maybe you don't have a wound," she replied.

"I do *too* have a wound."

"Becky, maybe not *everyone* has to have a wound."

"All God's children got wounds," I pouted.

"Look," she said with a wave of her hand, "You are welcome to borrow my childhood wound sometime."

"Could I really?" I asked, brightening. "Thank you, Gracie. You are my very best friend in the world."

"Don't mention it," she answered benevolently. "Now can we decide on what dessert to split?"

"I love you, do you know that?"

"I love you, too. Apple Crumb Pie or Chocolate-to-Die-For?"

"Chocolate-to-Die-For," we both said at once.

Becky Freeman is the author of
Lemonade Laughter & Laid-Back Joy.

I will not drag you along;

I will not leave you alone;

I will stand by you and have my hand

there for you to hold when you need to.

Piglet

A Friend ...

won't bring up your diet while you're both
    standing in front of a Baskin-Robbins.

won't laugh when your new permanent makes
    you look like you were struck by
    lightning ... twice.

will always take a double scoop of your dish at
    church potlucks ... no matter how life-
    threatening it may look.

will still eat your cookies ... even if the bottoms
    are burnt.

might join a gym with you, but she'll bring
    snacks to share when you're through.

will celebrate your birthday, but won't recall
    your exact age.

–Martha Bolton–

True friendship is forgetting what one has given,

and remembering what one has received.

Evelyn McCurdy

Dee Clark and Karla Yaconelli

Chitchat: Dee lives in the big city but she loves to ride rodeo.

Port of Safety

Dee Clark

A friend is a safe port in the midst of life's stormy seas. She welcomes you in and provides a place of rest and renewal. She accepts who you are and encourages who you are becoming. She allows for growth to come to you at God's pace and not her own. She is aware of her own brokenness and does not shy away from the brokenness of another.

There are few friendships that are able to weather the storms and changes that life brings. Karla is one of those friends. We quickly related on a soul level and discovered a similar passion for Jesus, life, and relationship. For eighteen years we have charted the course of life together. We have grown together, laughed together, and wept together. We have compared notes on parenting, marriage, the feminine journey, and spiritual pilgrimage. We have planned, schemed, and intentionalized some of the most amazing times together— times that have left an imprint of such magnitude that they changed me forever. I know Jesus better and I am able to live more freely out of the truth of His love as a result of the years of friendship that I've shared with Karla.

Dee Clark is a speaker and the coauthor of *Daughters and Dads*.

Think where man's glory most begins and ends,

and say my glory was I had such friends.

William Yeats

Left to Right: Jean Rohloff, Jill Rigby, Bunny Ferris, Cynthia
Lunceford, Coco Treppendahl, and Nanette Sammons

Chitchat: *While teaching a table manners lesson at her sons'
school, Jill hid in the cafeteria and screamed "NAPKIN CHECK,
FREEZE!" She proceeded to crawl under the tables and check their
laps for napkins.*

The Father's Porch

Jill Rigby

I have been blessed with an unlikely comradeship in a group of ladies who started out as strangers and who became sisters— sisters in Christ. We have gathered on Fridays for the past nine years and shared many sorrows, celebrated many victories, and prayed through many storms.

One summer while staying in the mountains, God gave me a vision that I couldn't wait to share with my sisters. It was an image of running breathlessly through the woods to discover a light shining from a cabin in the distance that beckoned, "Come near." Jesus stood at the gate to welcome me onto the porch where God sat in His rocking chair patiently waiting.

My sisters were as touched by the vision as I had been. When my birthday rolled around that year my sisters presented me with a box handsomely wrapped in brown paper. Their eyes danced with anticipation as I unwrapped the package. There it was down to the last detail: The Father's Porch. The cabin from the vision was in my hands. Even the Lord's rocking chair was sitting on the porch!

Jill Rigby is the originator of Manners of the Heart
educational series for children.

What a friend we have in Jesus!

All our sins and grief to bear!

Joseph M. Scriven

Yet I taught Ephraim to walk, taking them by their arms or taking them up

in My arms, but they did not know that I healed them. I drew with cords of a

man, with bands of love, and I was to them as

one who lifts up and eases the

yoke over their cheeks, and I bent down to them

and gently laid food before them.

Hosea 11:3-4, AMP

My Best Friend

Linda Evans Shepherd

My first memory of Jodie Ann started the only day it ever snowed in my childhood hometown of Beaumont, Texas. I was only a tot and bundled in so many layers I could hardly walk. Jodie Ann was only a baby, and she held her mother's neck tight, not daring to let her feet touch the cold, white fluff that covered the ground.

We were both too young to know that soon we would be best friends. Jodie grew into my favorite neighborhood playmate and we became inseparable. We spent hours setting up imaginary worlds for our miniature doll collection, discussing the fairy that surely lived in the knobby, live oak tree in my front yard, baking mud pies, and swinging as high as my backyard swing set would take us.

Then came that Christmas Day when Santa brought us each a walkie-talkie. After lunch, Jodie and I hid in the bushes, each in front of our own house, and pretended to be Agent 99 and Maxwell Smart. "Ninety-nine, I hear the evil KAOS agents are planning to rob the bank," I said into my radio.

"Let's pretend to be the KAOS agents!" Jodie said back.

"Okay, I've got dynamite. We'll blow up First National Bank's safe. No one will catch us on Christmas Day!"

Suddenly a male voice boomed out of our radios, "This is the Beaumont Police. We've heard your plans. We know who you are and where you are and we're coming to get you!"

Jodie and I jumped from our hiding places and ran to one another. "What should we do?" she asked.

"I bet they won't look for us under your bed!" I replied.

And that's where we spent the rest of Christmas Day. Apparently our hideout was a good one, because Jodie and I were never arrested.

We continued our childhood together filled with adventures and bike rides on sunny afternoons, and we continued to grow up.

All too soon we were doing high kicks to the band's beat with the high school drill team at halftime. Then, what seemed only a few moments later, Jodie announced to our college sorority that she would marry Bruce. When she walked down the aisle, I was her maid of honor. Later, when I married Paul, it was Jodie who stood beside me.

Today, while Jodie, the mother of two teenaged sons, works as a nurse in Beaumont, I am a writer living in Colorado with two teenagers as well. We're still friends, but we only see each other every few years.

Although my life's travels have taken me far beyond the warmth of family and friends, there is one childhood Friend who has stayed with me. It was this Friend who has comforted me in my most difficult days. It was this Friend who loved me when I was most unlovable and rejoiced with me when I celebrated my happiest moments.

I'll never forget the day we met. Even my mom was nervous as we waited for the doorbell to ring. *Why had I said that I wanted to meet him in the first place?* I wondered. But all too soon, my parents led the pastor into our living room. He sat down with me. "Linda, you checked on a card at church that you wanted to know Jesus."

I nodded, too afraid to speak.

"Do you believe He is God's Son?"

"Yes," I whispered.

"Do you believe He died on the cross in order to pay the penalty for your sins?"

"Yes."

"Do you believe He rose from the grave?"

I looked up into the pastor's eyes. "Yes, I do."

"Then pray this prayer with me." He said it first, then I repeated it.

"Dear God, I thank You for sending Your Son to die in my place. Please forgive me of my sins and come into my life. I give my life to you."

Tears slid down my cheeks. It had been such a simple prayer, but I could feel the presence of the living God slip into my very being.

I have felt God's presence within me ever since that night. God was with me when my young husband and I moved first to California then to Colorado. He was with me when my first child was injured in a car accident. He was with me through all my joys and through all my tears.

My friendship with God has been the very best part of my life. He completes who I am; He is someone I can trust no matter what circumstances I am going through. I depend on Him; I lean on Him; He turns my sorrows into joys. He loves me when I make mistakes and even when I'm not very lovable. He holds my hand when I'm afraid or confused.

Maybe you need a friend like that. Maybe you need a friend who will never leave you, who will stick closer than a brother. Maybe you need to feel loved in a way you've never realized love before. It does not matter who you are or what mistakes you've made, He already loves you and longs to be a part of your life. He gently calls your name and waits for you to recognize His voice. He longs to pull you close to His heart, to say, "I love you. All is forgiven. You are mine at last."

Perhaps you would allow me to introduce to you my best friend, Jesus. Just pray the simple pray that my pastor taught me and then start your own adventure with Him.

Linda Evans Shepherd is an author, speaker, president of Right to the Heart Ministries, and founder of the Advanced Writers and Speakers Association (AWSA).

Advanced Writers and Speakers Association

The Advanced Writers and Speakers Association (AWSA) is a professional support group made up of the top 10 percent of Christian women in both publishing and speaking. The group is made up of more than two hundred women, and is sponsored by the nonprofit ministry Right to the Heart. Their main event is the annual AWSA conference. AWSA also sponsors prayer teleconferences and the Golden Scroll Awards Banquet.

The umbrella ministry, Right to the Heart Ministries, serves a twofold purpose: to encourage, evangelize, and disciple our nation in daily, one-minute stories through a nationally syndicated radio show, Right to the Heart; and to equip, educate, encourage, and empower women's ministry leaders through connection with each other.

For more information on Right to the Heart Ministries or the AWSA, visit their website at www.righttotheheart.org.

MORE BOOKS FOR GROWING AND SHARING YOUR FAITH.

Becoming a Woman of Influence

Do you seek deep, connective relationships that will encourage you to grow? Discover principles for building solid relationships through simple steps to mentoring.

(Carol Kent)

Jesus Cares for Women

Do you have fears about sharing your faith? This unique guide gives you everything you need to overcome inhibitions and experience the joy of confidently sharing God's good news.

(Helene Ashker)

Jesus Changes Women

By looking at the lives of biblical women such as Deborah, Mary, and Hannah, you'll learn to root yourself in God's love, center your life on Christ, nourish your faith with Scripture, and enjoy fellowship.

(Helene Ashker)

Holy Habits

Holy Habits examines the character of God to show women how they can live each day intentionally and see their life as God sees it.

(Mimi Wilson and Shelly Cook Volkhardt)

To get your copies, visit your local bookstore, call 1-800-366-7788, or log on to www.navpress.com. Ask for a FREE catalog of NavPress products. Offer #BPA.

NAVPRESS

BRINGING TRUTH TO LIFE

www.navpress.com